Five-Minute Sermons for Children

by

Karen Berger, Carolyn Larsen, and Vicki Totel

illustrated by
Katherine Marlin

Cover by Katherine Marlin

Copyright © 1995 Shining Star

ISBN No. 0-382-30647-3

Standardized Subject Code TA ac

Printing No. 987654

Shining Star
A Division of Frank Schaffer Publications, Inc.
23740 Hawthorne Boulevard
Torrance, CA 90505-5927

Unless otherwise indicated, the New International Version of the Bible was used in preparing the activities in this book.

DEDICATION

To all those caring teachers, pastors, and parents who want more than anything to help children understand and apply God's truths to their lives. May the Spirit of Truth speak through each of you as you use these sermons.

TABLE OF CONTENTS

Shining Star, Copyright © 1995

0-382-30647-3

TO PARENTS AND TEACHERS

We have so many wonderful truths to teach our children, but they just don't seem to listen when we "preach at" them! Someone once said that the worst thing we could ever do is to bore our children with God's Word. This book provides interesting, attention-keeping, brief sermons or devotionals for children to guarantee that they won't be bored. Instead, they will learn important truths from God's Word through true stories, object lessons, and examples that relate to their everyday lives.

Each sermon is based on a Bible verse or passage which may be read aloud to the children to make it clear to them that these are lessons from God. Each one also includes a list of materials needed to illustrate the theme.

Here are some guidelines for presenting these sermons to your children:

1. Each of these sermons is intended to last about five minutes. Keep as close to that time limit as possible. Children's attention spans are brief, but they can learn a lot in a few minutes. Depend on the Holy Spirit to apply these truths to their lives after you have shared the information.

2. Make sure you have eye contact with the children. Don't give all your attention to the best or worst listeners. Rather, try to look directly at each child at some time during the talk.

3. Gather any materials you need and have them organized and in their correct places before you begin talking. It's usually better not to pass items around to the children while you are talking. If you have something to give the children, hand it out at the end of the sermon.

4. Whenever possible, replace the true stories and illustrations with similar experiences in your own life. This will make your sermons come alive for the children.

5. Read each sermon several times and practice saying it before presenting it. Do not read the sermon to the children. If you must use notes, print them on small cards which will not be obvious when you hold them in your hands.

6. As you prepare each sermon, pray about your presentation of it and pray for the children who will be hearing it.

7. End each sermon with a simple prayer, asking God to apply the truth in the life of each child. Prayers are not provided with the sermons, since you will want to compose your own prayer for each specific group of children.

The sermons in this book are arranged alphabetically by topic. They include seasonal themes as well as themes on values and Christian living. Use them as children's sermons in your church worship service and as devotionals for children's church, clubs, and parties. They are also excellent for tying together what children have studied in Sunday School if you have a group time at the end of your Sunday School hour. Parents may want to use them as family devotions at home.

ADVENT
Galatians 4:4a

Materials Needed: Advent calendar

Have you ever helped your family plan a vacation? For months before it was time for the trip, you and your parents may have looked through brochures and information about the place where you were going. Perhaps you and your mom wrote for literature about the place. Maybe you talked with other people who had been there and got inside information on what to do while you were there.

Planning a trip is almost as much fun as actually taking the trip. As you make more and more plans, and the time for the trip gets closer and closer, you get more and more excited. When it is only a few days before the trip, your mom does laundry and you begin to pack suitcases. Dad makes sure the car is all ready to travel a long way. You find someone to take care of your pets and water the plants and take in the mail. Finally, you are through getting ready and it is time to go on the trip.

I brought something with me today that helps us all get ready for a very special event. You may have one of these in your house. This is an advent calendar. Advent season begins four weeks before Christmas and continues right up to Christmas Eve. This colorful calendar has a little door to open for every day of the month of December. When we start opening these doors we start thinking more and more about Christmas. The preparations for Christmas can keep us very busy. We send Christmas cards and go shopping for gifts. We put up a Christmas tree and decorate the house. Then there is the baking and the dinner to think about. Usually there are Christmas programs at church and school. My, it's a busy time of year, isn't it?

Do you know what else the advent calendar can do for us? It can remind us every day of the season that as we are doing all the fun things to get ready for this wonderful holiday, we should remember that we are really getting ready to celebrate the birth of Jesus. Many advent calendars have little pictures behind the doors that are opened–animals that might have been in the stable where Jesus was born, angels such as those who announced His birth to the shepherds, a little baby in a manger, Baby Jesus.

This Christmas season as you open the doors of your advent calendar, remember every day to thank God that Jesus came to earth. Enjoy all the preparations and excitement as you get ready for Christmas, but don't forget why we are celebrating the wonderful holiday.

by Carolyn Larsen

...ining Star, Copyright © 1995

0-382-30647-3

ANGELS
Acts 12:1-18

Have you ever seen an angel? I don't mean the angel that you put on top of your Christmas tree. What do you think a real angel would look like? (Let children offer suggestions.)

There are many stories in the Bible about angels. Sometimes when they appeared they looked like what you have been describing–dressed all in white with a bright light surrounding them. But sometimes they just looked like ordinary everyday people, and it might be hard to even know they were angels. God sent angels to people in Bible times to protect them, give them instructions, make announcements to them, and comfort them.

The apostle Peter was protected by an angel when he was in prison. Peter hadn't done anything wrong except teach about Jesus. He shouldn't have been in trouble for that, should he? But he was. Peter's friends prayed for God to protect him. God sent an angel to help Peter escape from prison. The angel appeared one night in Peter's cell when he was sleeping. "Get up!" the angel said. Peter was chained between two guards, but the angel made the chains fall off Peter's wrists, and suddenly he was free.

"Follow me," the angel said. Sixteen soldiers were guarding Peter in a locked prison, and they wouldn't let him just walk out the door. But God made the guards not even notice that Peter was walking past them. The angel led him right up to the prison door and no guards even tried to stop them! The prison doors opened all by themselves, and Peter thought he was dreaming! The angel led him out to the street, then disappeared! Peter was free, and God had used an angel to make it happen!

Does God still send angels to help us today? Yes, but we may meet angels and think they are regular people because they look just like us. A little girl named Mallory went to a big zoo with her family. It was a very busy day; there were lots of people walking around. Mallory and her family walked along slowly looking at the animals. Mallory walked more slowly than everyone else. She was climbing on rocks and jumping, and pretty soon she was a little bit behind them. When her family turned a corner, Mallory didn't notice which way they went. When she realized they were gone, she got frightened. She began running along the sidewalk, looking for her parents. Her parents were looking for her too, but Mallory was running in the opposite direction! It might have been a long time before they found each other, but someone came along to help Mallory. Was it an angel sent to protect her? A lady saw Mallory running and crying, and she took her to the zoo office, where she waited until her Mom and Dad came to get her. Mallory's parents were so thankful. They felt the lady might have been an angel that God had sent.

Let's thank God for His special angel helpers who are constantly watching over us and helping us.

by Carolyn Larsen

Shining Star, Copyright © 1995

0-382-30647-3

AVOIDING WRONG
1 Corinthians 10:12-13

or use pictures of

Materials Needed: Fishing equipment (lures, hooks, a reel, pole, or a fishing net)

Anybody here like to go fishing? Have you ever caught a fish? Even if you've never caught one, there's a lesson we can learn from fishing.

Once there was a boy named Jason who loved to fish. He could hardly lift his tackle box. There was enough equipment in it to supply a whole dock of fishermen. He was so proud of his lures. His aunt had bought him two lures that glowed in the dark! He had saved his allowance and bought other supplies, a few at a time.

As he walked toward the pond one morning, he just knew it would be a great day for fishing. The sky was overcast, the air was crisp, and he just felt that the fish would be biting. Jason spent most of the morning fishing. He put bait on the hook, cast it out, waited awhile, and then reeled in a big one (well, it sure felt like a big one when he pulled it from the water). He used corn for bait, sometimes cheese, and even a big juicy worm from his backyard. He waited for a nibble on the line. It was relaxing to be by the pond. He looked into the ripples of the water and daydreamed.

Something his Sunday School teacher had said made him think of his fishing gear as he stared into the water. Mr. Oakley had said that God loves to talk to boys when they're fishing, because that's when they can be quiet and relax their minds. Mr. Oakley was talking about avoiding wrong things. "Temptation is often like a lure," he said. "It looks inviting and good, but when we bite, we find it's only a hook to trap us and cause us to sin." Jason knew from other lessons in Sunday School that Satan is the one who tries to make us sin. He makes sin look harmless and fun.

Shining Star, Copyright © 1995

0-382-30647-3

Jason laid down his pole and opened his tackle box. As he looked over its contents he thought, "Mr. Oakley was right!" There were bright colored lures, some that looked just like worms. Some of them smelled like fish bait and some felt all squishy. Jason even had some that would wiggle and rattle in the water. The advertisements had said that this bait tasted better. He wondered who had tasted the bait to be sure. Jason had everything to make a fish think he was getting a good snack.

(Read 1 Corinthians 10:13 aloud in an easy-to-understand version of the Bible.) Temptation to do something wrong happens to everyone, so when you are tempted don't think you're the only one who has ever felt this way. Other people have resisted temptation, and you can too. God will help you resist doing wrong. He promises to give you the help you need when you ask Him. He may bring other people into your life to help you through the temptation. He may even use your mind by helping you to remember a Bible verse or story you have studied.

Jason started thinking of things he could do to keep from doing wrong. It sounded easy to just avoid doing wrong things, but he knew that it wasn't always as easy as it sounds. It is easier to sin sometimes than to be strong and not sin. He thought it was probably smart to know the situations that cause you trouble, to be aware of your weak spots. When they come up, they should be like a yellow light that tells you to be cautious. He already knew he needed to pray for God's help to do right and that he needed to have friends that would help him do right things. Jason took a moment to ask God to help him.

Do you ask God every day to help you do right and avoid wrong? That's something we all need to do!

by Vicki Totel

THE BIBLE
2 Timothy 3:10-17

The word *Bible* means "books." The Bible is like a library with different kinds of books in it. There are books of law, history, biographies of many people, poetry, and letters from people to other people.

What do you know about the Bible? What is the shortest book? (2 John–It has only 13 verses.) What is the longest book? (Psalms–It has 150 chapters.) What is the shortest verse in the Bible? (John 11:35–"Jesus wept.")

Some of the books of the Bible have very funny sounding names, such as Habakkuk, Zephaniah, and Haggai. Perhaps if we spent more time with our Bibles, some of these books wouldn't seem so strange to us. Sometimes it's hard to find a certain verse in the Bible, isn't it? It isn't necessary to know each exact location. In fact, one of the most used pages of your Bible should be the index page, which tells the page on which each book begins.

The Bible was written for you and me–for each one of us. When we hear it read or we read it ourselves, we should remember that God is speaking to us individually. We are responsible for what we read and hear. Paul, in his letter to Timothy, told him that the holy Scriptures are able to make us wise for salvation through faith in Christ Jesus and that the Scriptures are useful in teaching us how to be equipped for every good work. The Bible cannot do this for us unless we read it. Begin today. Don't try to read the whole Bible at once, just a little at a time. Start with one book from God's great library. Read a few verses each day to discover what God wants to say to you.

by Karen Berger

0-382-30647-3

THE BEST PRESENT EVER
John 3:16

Materials Needed: A large, beautifully wrapped gift box addressed to you. Inside the box put a piece of paper with these words on it: "Eternal life. Love, God."

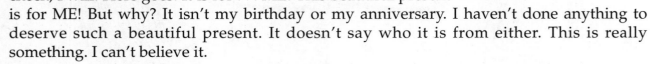

(Leave the package at the front of the room so it will be there when you come up to tell the story.) Boys and girls, look at this gift. I don't know if I have ever seen a more beautiful package. It has such lovely wrapping paper and look at this pretty bow. Here's a tag. It must say who this gift is for. I wonder who it could be? Shall I look and see who it is for? (Let the children encourage you to check the name tag.) Well, all right, if you want me to check, I will. Here goes. It is for . . . ME! This beautiful present is for ME! But why? It isn't my birthday or my anniversary. I haven't done anything to deserve such a beautiful present. It doesn't say who it is from either. This is really something. I can't believe it.

But I wonder, who is it from? Who would give me this beautiful package? Is it from you? No? Well, is it from you then? How about you? (Go to different children and ask them the question.) Well, I just don't know who it is from.

I also don't know what is in this pretty package. It must be something really special. Maybe it's pretty clothes or fancy jewelry. Or it might be some new books. I do love to read. I wonder what it is? (Look at children and pretend they encourage you to open it, even if they don't say anything.) What? You want me to open it? Oh, I don't know if I should. Well, maybe it would be all right. It is addressed to me. OK, I'll open it.

(Tear off ribbon and paper carefully.) Here we go. I'm sooo excited. I can't wait to see what it is. (Open box.) The only thing in here is a piece of paper. It says, "Eternal life. Love, God." (Excitedly explain.) I know what this means. This really is the best gift ever. You see, none of us could know God or have eternal life in heaven with Him because we are sinners. God doesn't allow sin in heaven. It's like I was on one side of a big canyon and God was on the other side. There was no way for me to get across and join Him. But God loves me so much that He sent His Son, Jesus, to earth to die on the cross for my sins. If I believe in what Jesus did for me, I can have eternal life. I can live forever in heaven. Jesus is like a bridge across that big canyon. That's my gift. Isn't that great? What a wonderful gift.

Want to know the best part? This gift is not just for me. God sent Jesus to earth for everyone. If you believe that Jesus died for your sins, you can have eternal life too. So, I guess this package is really for all of us.

If you want to know more about this wonderful gift, talk to me or your parents or Sunday School teacher later. Any of us would love to help you learn about Jesus.

by Carolyn Larsen

0-382-30647-3

BROWN SUGAR BLESSINGS
Luke 6:38

Materials Needed: Bag of brown sugar (not pressed together), measuring cup that will hold all the brown sugar when it is pressed down (premeasure this, then fluff the sugar before the sermon so it looks like more sugar than should fit in the cup), spoon, chocolate chip cookies for all the children

When I was a little girl (boy), I always loved it when my mom baked chocolate chip cookies. It was my favorite cookie, but there was an extra benefit to that baking time. That was when Mom got out the brown sugar to put in the cookie batter. She would always let me have a spoonful of brown sugar, just for me. That is a sweet memory, letting brown sugar melt in my mouth while I sat and watched Mom mixing up cookies. Soon the smell of baking cookies filled the house, and my mouth would be watering for the warm cookies.

Today I want to show you something I have learned about brown sugar. It's actually a lesson about how much God loves me. Look at this bag of brown sugar I brought with me. It's soft and fluffy. There's quite a bit of sugar in the bag, isn't there? Now watch as I put some of this brown sugar in a measuring cup and press it down firmly with my spoon. See, when I press it down, there is room for more sugar. (Put more sugar in measuring cup.) Now I can press this down, and there is room for more brown sugar. (Keep adding sugar until it's gone and the cup is full.) Isn't it amazing that all that brown sugar fit into this little cup?

What spiritual lesson can we learn from this? Listen to this Bible verse from Luke: "Give, and it will be given to you. A good measure, pressed down, shaken together and running over, will be poured into your lap." (Luke 6:38) I can do many things for God. I can tell stories that help you children learn about Him, I can sing in the choir, I can pray for other people, I can share all the abilities He gave me with His people. But no matter how much I do for Him, He gives more back to me. I just can't out give God. When I give myself to Him, the good things He gives me just keep coming and coming. When I think He has given me all the friends and good times and nice things and answers to prayers that He can possibly give, He gives me more! Like the brown sugar pressed in this cup, God gives us more than we think we could ever receive.

I have something for you to help you remember this "Brown sugar verse"–chocolate chip cookies! (Pass out cookies.) As you eat these, remember that the more you give to God, the more He gives to you!

by Carolyn Larsen

CHRISTMAS
Luke 2:1-20

Materials Needed: A bag of items appropriate for a child's birthday party (hats, noisemakers, balloons, banners, etc.)

If we were going to celebrate someone's birthday today, what would we need for the party? (As the children mention items, take them out of the bag.) How do you like to celebrate your birthday? (Wait for several responses.) Have you ever asked your parents what they did to celebrate the day you were born–your "birth" day? (Wait briefly for responses.)

When Jesus was born, there was quite a party! The animals of the stable were already there. Do you think they knew something special was happening? The animals might have been some of the noisemakers at Jesus' birthday party! Were there bright lights and decorations? Who else ever had the whole sky shining for his birthday with an especially bright star in the east? There was lots of heavenly music too. Angels sang and told shepherds about the party in the stable. What a way to receive a party invitation! And what a birthday song that must have been!

Let's celebrate Jesus' birthday this year by showing others the love of God in us. When you go home, make a birthday card for Jesus. Ask the members of your family to sign it with you. Then place the card on your dinner table as a reminder of Jesus' birth. Sing "Happy Birthday, Jesus," before your dinner on Christmas day.

Let's sing "Happy Birthday" to Jesus right now.

by Karen Berger

0-382-30647-3

DISAPPOINTMENT
John 11:1-44

Have you ever wanted something to happen so much that it was all you thought about? Maybe you prayed and asked God to let it happen. Maybe you even remembered that there is a Bible verse that says you can ask anything in His name and He will do it for you. Did it happen? If it did, I'm sure you were very happy and thankful to God. If it didn't, were you disappointed? Did you wonder why God didn't answer your prayer. Listen to this story about a girl who was disappointed.

Kara loved to play volleyball. She had her parents put up a net in her backyard, and she practiced everyday. When school started, Kara tried out for the sixth grade volleyball team. There were many good players at the tryouts. Some were taller than Kara and some could jump higher, but none of them wanted to be on the team more than Kara did.

Kara prayed that God would help her play her very best at the tryouts and make the team. Kara really believed God would make sure she got on the team. Tryouts went OK. She felt that she played pretty well. Waiting for the list of the girls who made the team to be posted was really hard. When the list came out, Kara felt terrible. She hadn't made it!

At first Kara was angry at God for not answering her prayer. Then she was just disappointed. She didn't understand why He hadn't let her make the team. It was hard to understand.

Mary and Martha, two sisters in the Bible knew how it feels to be disappointed with God. They and their brother Lazarus were good friends of Jesus. They knew that Jesus healed sick people and made blind people see. They knew He could do wonderful things. So when Lazarus got very sick, Mary and Martha sent for Jesus. They said, "Your friend that You love is sick. He needs You!" Wouldn't you think Jesus would hurry right to their house? He didn't. In fact, by the time Jesus got to their house, Lazarus was dead.

Mary and Martha were so disappointed. They said, "Jesus, if You had been here our brother would still be alive." Jesus felt badly for them, but He wanted them to trust Him. Their disappointment turned to joy and a stronger faith in God when Jesus raised their brother from the dead. Everyone who saw the miracle knew that Jesus had wonderful power from God.

Sometimes we understand why God doesn't answer our prayers the way we want Him to. Maybe in Kara's case, being on the volleyball team would have been too much for her, causing her grades to slip. We don't always know why He does or doesn't do the things we ask Him to do. The bottom line is, we have to believe that God loves us. He wants the very best for each of us, and He knows what the best is, even when we don't. So trust Him, even when you are disappointed. Remember that He loves you very much.

by Carolyn Larsen

DOING MY PART
1 Corinthians 12:14-25

Materials Needed: Sports squeezer bottle filled with water on a table at the front of the room. If possible, wear a jogging suit or at least a sweatband around your head.

(Come in as if you have been jogging for a while.) "Whew! I'm beat. I really enjoy jogging. It feels good to exercise. I've got these great feet and legs. See? (Hold up a leg at a time and wiggle your foot at the kids.) I have two of each. My leg muscles are very strong because of jogging and they really do a wonderful job. (Jog in place for a few steps.) And my feet–well, I just can't say enough about my feet. They hit the pavement time after time with all my weight crashing down on them, and they just keep right on going as long as I want them to. I think so much of my feet that I bought these expensive running shoes to put on them. I really think they deserve the very best.

Of course, jogging makes me thirsty. A big gulp of ice cold water would really taste good. Yes sir, that would really hit the spot! (Notice cup of water on the table.) Why, look over here. There's a cup, and it looks like it might have ice water in it. I'm just going to go right over and have a big drink of that. (Walk to table, but do not pick up cup.) OK, I'll have a drink now. I said, I'll have a drink now. What is going on here? I don't seem to be able to pick up this cup. Something is wrong with my arm. Wait, what was that? Did you all hear something? It, uh, sounds like my arm is trying to say something to me. Excuse me. (Hold arm up to ear as if listening to it.)

My arm says that it and my hand have decided not to pick up the cup. They say that since I'm so proud of my feet and legs, they can pick up the cup for me.

I guess my arm is jealous of my feet and legs. Listen, Mr. Arm, you aren't any less important than my feet or legs. I need all of you. If my body doesn't get food and water, I can't be healthy, or even stay alive! Then it won't matter how good my legs and feet are. All you body parts have to be happy with who you are; you must work together as a team or my body won't be any good at all.

(Listen to arm again.) What? You understand now? Great, let's get that drink." (Pick up cup and take a big drink.)

You know, this was a good lesson for all of us. God wants us to be happy with who we are. We should do what we are good at and not waste our energy wishing we could be someone else or have a different job. Every job is important, especially in our work for the Lord. Whatever you can do for Him, whether you pick up trash in the parking lot or sing a solo or preach a sermon, helps His body, the church. Each one is needed and important, just like each part of the body. Remember, there aren't any little parts in God's work.

by Carolyn Larsen

EASTER
Matthew 28:1-10

Materials Needed: A calendar for Lent and Easter (Mark the forty days before Easter and the days of Holy Week, if appropriate for your group.)

Do you know how the date on the calendar is set for Easter? (Wait for children's ideas.) Traditionally Easter is said to be on the first Sunday after the first full moon that comes on or after the first day of spring (approximately March 21). It's not important that we know how this date is calculated for our calendar, but it **is** important that we know why we celebrate it.

Lent is the season that begins forty days before Easter, not counting Sundays. (Show the calendar.) During Lent the days are "lengthening" in daylight hours. We say that the days are getting longer. Each day still has twenty-four hours, but there is more daylight than there is in the winter. Because of more sunshine, light, and warmth for the earth, there is more activity in nature. That's when flowers begin to bud, trees begin to sprout their leaves, and lots of animals are born. During Lent we should remember what Jesus did for us by His death on the cross. We need to remember that He died for our sins. A lot of people use this time to break old, bad habits and to learn new, good ones. It's a time to help us remember how much Jesus loves us.

When Easter comes, the earth appears to be coming back to life after winter. As Christians, we celebrate Jesus' coming back to life after His death on the cross. Every Sunday is a little celebration of Jesus' resurrection. But Easter is a BIG celebration of Jesus living again. There are many ways we can remember His love for us. One special way is to show Jesus how much we love Him as we worship together. As we do that today, let's thank Him for His love.

by Karen Berger

ENCOURAGING OTHERS
1 Thessalonians 5:11

Have you ever been discouraged? It doesn't feel very good, does it? I have a story for you today about a boy who was discouraged.

Marcus sat on the wooden bench, hunched over, drawing lines in the dirt with a stick. He wasn't talking to anyone and none of the other kids were paying any attention to him. They were all busy with their game. All the other boys and girls were playing baseball. Marcus wanted to play, but when they chose up teams no one wanted him because Marcus didn't play baseball very well. His baseball glove lay in the dirt, and Marcus did his best to act like he didn't care. But inside, Marcus wanted to cry.

After a few minutes an older boy named David came over to talk to Marcus. "Hey Marcus," David said, "I feel bad that we didn't choose you to play."

"Oh, that's OK," Marcus mumbled, but he didn't really mean it. "I don't play so well, I would probably make my team lose."

"Well, I can help you with that. Meet me here at the field after supper tonight. I can teach you how to play baseball," David said.

That evening David and Marcus practiced throwing and catching. David showed Marcus how to hit the ball and how to run the bases. They didn't just work that night; they practiced every night for two weeks.

Two weeks later, when all the kids gathered at the baseball field and began choosing teams for another baseball game, Marcus was there. Suddenly, he heard David call his name! "Marcus, you're on my team." The other kids on the team started complaining. David just ignored the complaints and went right on choosing players.

David's team was up to bat first, and he chose Marcus to be the first batter. David quietly walked over to Marcus and said, so no one else could hear, "I know you can do this. Just do what I taught you."

Marcus' confidence started to come back. He felt good that David believed in him. Even though he could hear some of the kids in the field laughing and making fun of him, Marcus stepped up to the plate and lifted the bat up over his shoulder, ready for the first pitch. The first ball came at him. He swung the bat, but missed. Some of his teammates moaned, and some of the fielders laughed out loud. But Marcus looked at David who smiled and held one thumb straight up in the air.

Marcus missed the second pitch too. Some of the fielders rolled on the ground, laughing. Marcus turned back to the pitcher, took a deep breath, and raised his bat. The ball came at him and Marcus hit it! He ran all the way to second base.

Don't you feel happy for Marcus? So did David, his encourager. We all need to be encouraged once in a while. We all need to be told "You can do it. Keep on trying. I believe in you!"

We need to encourage other people too. God tells us in the Bible, "Therefore encourage one another and build each other up, just as in fact you are doing" (1 Thessalonians 5:11). Do you know someone who needs to hear that someone believes in him? If you get a chance to be an encourager, do it! And remember to thank anyone who encourages you.

by Carolyn Larsen

ETERNAL LIFE
John 3:16; Romans 6:23

Materials Needed: Pictures of a baby, a teen, a middle-aged person, and a very old person (These need not be all the same people.)

(Hold up picture of baby.) I have a picture here of a little baby. Isn't he cute? What happens to a little baby if he is healthy and eats properly? He grows. (Show picture of teen.) In a few years the little baby becomes a teenager. His body grows bigger and his mind becomes more advanced. What happens after this? (Hold up picture of middle-aged person.) A few years later, the teen grows into a middle-aged person of about fifty years. That's a long time, isn't it? But look at this picture. (Hold up picture of old person.) How old do you think this person is? It's hard to imagine living that long, isn't it? In a few years, this person's life will be over. No one lives forever. Sooner or later everyone's life will end.

But wait! I have some great news for you. Your life on earth will end, but you don't have to die forever. God has a wonderful plan for anyone who chooses to follow it. Anyone who does will be able to come to heaven and live with Him. Here is the plan: God can't allow sin in His perfect heaven, but we are all sinners. If He let sin into heaven, it would be like putting a rotten peach in a basket full of good peaches. What happens? Pretty soon the rottenness spreads and all the peaches are touched by the rottenness.

Here's how God solved that problem. Jesus came to earth and died for our sins. Jesus is God's Son and He never sinned. When He died, it was totally for us. If we believe that Jesus died, tell Him we are sorry for our sins, and that we want Jesus to come live in our hearts, we can have eternal life. That's because our sin is gone as far as God is concerned. He doesn't see it anymore because Jesus took care of it for us. When the time comes for our earthly bodies to die, we can go to heaven to live with God forever!

by Carolyn Larsen

0-382-30647-3

FAITH
Ephesians 2:8-9

Materials Needed: A gift-wrapped package which contains candies or small items you can share with the children

Here is a lovely package. (Describe it, building with excitement as to what might be inside. Shake it, rattle it, look for a name tag, etc.) Well, I know who wrapped it, and you'll just have to trust me that I know there is something inside for all of you!

Our faith in God is a lot like this gift. Ephesians 2:8 tells us that our belief in God is a gift from Him. (Read the verse aloud.) We cannot really give a gift to ourselves, can we? In the same way we cannot give the gift of salvation to ourselves. The Bible also tells us that we cannot work for our salvation or trust in God. (Read Ephesians 2:9.) People work for a paycheck, but a gift is given because of love. Our faith comes from believing what Jesus did for us when He died on the cross and came back to life. God gave His Son Jesus as a gift to us so that we could have eternal life with Him. All God asks of us is to accept His gift. The gift is there–all we need to do is have the faith to accept it.

If we let this package sit on a shelf and never open it and enjoy it, then it is just a decoration and would not be very useful. The same is true of our faith in God. We need to use His gift of salvation by sharing His love with others. We show to God and to others that we are using God's gift to us by loving Him and others. God doesn't want us to miss His love for us. That's one of the reasons He gave us such a special gift through Jesus.

Oh, yes, let's open this gift and share it together! (Hand out the items inside the box.)

by Karen Berger

0-382-30647-3

FORGIVENESS

11-16-09
M. Jones

Luke 15:11-31

When was the last time you did something you thought was right, only to find out later that it really wasn't a very smart move at all? Sometimes our decisions aren't necessarily the best decisions. We may even have to ask someone to forgive us for a bad decision we made. And we can't always see our mistake until later when we think back about our actions.

The story of the Prodigal Son is one that clearly shows forgiveness. Two brothers were helping their father on the farm. The younger son made some decisions that he thought at the time were right for him. He asked his father for the money that would be coming to him some day. Then he selfishly left home. He thought he was ready for anything the world had to offer.

He made many friends and lived in a land far away from his family. He spent his money on foolish luxuries instead of necessities. Do you know what a luxury is? (Something you want, but don't really need.) Do you know what a necessity is? (Something you need.) How are they different? A car might be a necessity to some people, but a fancy, expensive, bright red sports car with all the latest gadgets is a luxury. (Give other examples you can think of that apply to the children you are teaching.)

The younger son had lots of friends until his money ran out. His careless life-style left him without money or friends to help him. He had to get a job feeding pigs. Now this didn't exactly seem like a job for someone who thought he had made such a good decision. It turns out that he had made a few mistakes along the way. Now he was so hungry he wanted to eat the food that was meant for the pigs.

One day the boy thought about the men that worked for his father. He remembered that they always had plenty to eat and were never hungry as he was. He thought for awhile and then made another decision. He decided to return home and ask his father for his forgiveness. The boy was willing to be a servant for his father if only he would forgive his son's foolish mistakes.

What happiness and joy filled the father's heart as he saw his son coming home! He was so thrilled to see the boy, the father hugged and kissed him and made plans for a big welcome-home party. The son begged for his father's forgiveness. "I'm not even worthy to be your son," he cried. The father was full of forgiveness for him. His son had been lost, but now he was back where he belonged.

When we look back at some decisions we have made that didn't turn out to be so good, we need to remember that God forgives us just as the father forgave his son. That's because He loves us.

by Vicki Totel

FRUIT OF THE SPIRIT
Galatians 5:22-23

Materials Needed: A package of flower or vegetable seeds

(Read Galatians 5:22-23.) The fruit of the Spirit are characteristics in a Christian's life; in other words, it is the way you live your life. You can't go down to the grocery store and buy a bag of peace or a pound of patience. You can't order self-control from the catalog or borrow gentleness from your best friend. These are all things that come from within. The Bible calls them fruit because like fruit these characteristics start out tiny and grow—as you learn to live for Jesus.

In the spring stores start selling little packages of seeds. (Show students a package of seeds.) The seeds are so tiny, you have to shake the bag to see if there are any in the package. How could these tiny, dried-up things do anything besides just sit there in the package? If you place them in some warm soil, water them a bit, and wait for the sun to shine on them, the seeds will sprout. After a while the sprouts will start to push up through the soil. Before long, little green plants grow from the seeds that didn't seem to have any value before. The fragile little plants need to be protected from storms, animals, and weeds so they will grow big and strong. Then blossoms will appear and they will grow too. As the plants grow, the gardener is happy because his work has been successful.

0-382-30647-3

If you have Jesus in your heart, the Holy Spirit is in you too. The Spirit wants you to have these qualities and attitudes in your life as a way of showing other people God's love. He wants you to be loving, patient, and full of joy. He wants you to be gentle and kind and have self-control. You can have goodness and peace too. God will help these things to grow in your life if you trust Him.

The more you get to know Jesus through Bible study and prayer, the more you will be like Him. As you grow up and try to be like Jesus, you will find that His love, joy, and peace will become part of you. Your patience, kindness, and goodness will be seen by others. Faithfulness, gentleness, and self-control will be words other people use to describe you. Just as soil, water, and sunshine help plants grow, Bible reading, prayer, and living like Jesus help you grow into a better Christian.

The Bible says when we see the way a person behaves, we can see whether or not he loves Jesus. Those who are always hateful and impatient and unkind are not acting like Jesus wants them to.

Do you want to live a life that pleases God and points other people to Him? Do you want to have love, joy, peace, patience, kindness, goodness, faithfulness, gentleness, and self-control? The Holy Spirit wants all Christians to have these qualities growing in them. Let's ask Jesus to help us today.

by Vicki Totel

0-382-30647-3

GOD IS WITH YOU
Hebrews 13:5b-6a

Materials Needed: A pair of good shoes (such as ones worn on Sunday) and a pair of everyday shoes (such as sneakers that look used or worn)

Once there was a little boy named Ryan. He loved baseball, soccer, collecting sports cards, and spending a whole day fishing with his best friend. He had a pet dog and cat that he enjoyed playing with too.

Ryan hated thunderstorms, especially at night. When the rain started pounding down, and the thunder was crashing all around, and lightning flashes filled the room, do you know what Ryan did? He grabbed his pillow and headed for Mom and Dad's bedroom. He didn't wake them up or climb into their bed. He just lay down on the floor next to their bed. Sometimes he just waited until the storm was over, and then he went back to his own room. But sometimes he fell asleep there and didn't wake up until morning.

One morning after an especially noisy thunderstorm, Mom woke up and noticed Ryan sleeping on the floor beside her bed. When he woke up she asked him, "Why does it make you feel better to be in our room during a thunderstorm? You don't wake us up."

Ryan answered, "I just don't like to be alone when there is a storm. I feel better if someone is with me."

"Did you forget that God is with you all the time?" Mom asked. "He never leaves you. It's OK that you come in our room when you are afraid, but remember that God is with you too. He will help you not be afraid, if you ask Him."

"I guess I mostly think about God on Sundays," Ryan said. "I forget that He's with me all the time."

Boys and girls, do you sometimes forget about God except on Sundays? (Hold up "Sunday" shoes.) These are someone's good "Sunday" shoes. They are worn only on Sunday when the person goes to church. Here's another pair of shoes. (Hold up sneakers.) These are "everyday" shoes. They are worn almost every day. See how worn they are? They are very comfortable because they are so broken in.

Which pair of shoes makes you think of God? "Sunday" shoes? After all, they go to church on Sundays, and they are nice and clean. But you know what? It's the comfy sneakers that make me think of God. Church is not the only place you can find God. He is with you every single day, like these sneakers. You don't just take God out on Sundays, like these shoes (hold up good shoes), then put Him away after church until the next Sunday. God is always with you, through thunderstorms, sunny days, when you're sleeping, when you're in school–all the time! Doesn't that make you feel good? You can talk to Him whenever you want, and He is there to help you with anything that happens. (Read Hebrews 13:5b-6a aloud.)

by Carolyn Larsen

GODLY SPEECH
James 3:10

Dane

Materials Needed: New tube of toothpaste, paper plate, plastic knife

(As you say each unkind word or phrase in the following talk, squeeze a big squirt of toothpaste on a paper plate. By the time you are finished with these hurtful words you will have a big pile of toothpaste.) Did you know that the words you say may hurt other people? Maybe you are playing with a friend and you don't get your way. Your friend insists on playing the game his way, and you get very angry. So you angrily shout, "I don't like you; you're mean!" or "I'm going home. I don't want to be your friend anymore" or even "I hate you!"

Perhaps you and a friend see a person you don't know, and you whisper to each other, "Look at her funny hair" or "Yuk, what ugly clothes!" Hurtful words may pile up in a person's heart. (Hold up toothpaste pile on plate.) Unkind words like these can really hurt another person. They can make the other person feel ugly or sad. *How do you think they made the person feel?* When you know that your words have hurt someone else, have you wished you could *had not said them?* just take them back? (Choose one of the older children from the group to come up and help you.) Would you help me by putting this toothpaste back in the tube while I finish talking? Here's a knife to help you. (Let the child work on this while you continue talking.)

Of course, when you have hurt someone with your words, *what can you do?* you *can* say you are sorry for what you have said. The other person may say you are forgiven. Even if your apology is sincere, the hurt and ugly feelings you have caused down inside that person will still be there. That's why it is good to think before you speak. Think about how your friend will feel about what you say.

(Turn to your helper.) Do you have the toothpaste back in the tube yet? What? It won't go back in? Oh dear! Well, you know what? This toothpaste is a lot like the unkind words we sometimes say. We can't take them back.

When you have hurt someone with your unkind words, you can say you are sorry, but you can't really take back the way you have made that person feel.

The Bible tells us in James 3:10 that it isn't right for good words and bad words to come out of the same mouth. We should use our mouths to praise God and say only kind and ~~encouraging~~ *good* words to our friends.

by Carolyn Larsen

GOD PROVIDES FOR US
Matthew 14:22-32

Materials Needed: In advance, assemble a "sea in a bottle" by removing the label from an empty two-liter soda pop bottle. After rinsing it out, fill it half full of water. Tightly crumple a ball of foil about the size of a dime. Drop it in the water. Mix some baby oil with blue food coloring, enough to fill the remainder of the bottle. Place the cap on tightly. After the oil and water have separated, the bottle may be tipped gently from side to side to look like the waves of the sea. For bigger waves, tip the bottle farther from side to side. As you tell about Jesus walking on the water, use your "sea in a bottle." The foil inside will be tossed about like the disciples' boat.

After teaching all day, Jesus sent His disciples out in a boat to go to the other side of the lake while He went by Himself to pray. That evening a storm came up. The wind blew and the waves rocked the boat from side to side. Jesus was walking on the water to reach the boat and His disciples. The disciples were frightened when they saw Him, thinking it was a ghost coming toward them. Jesus immediately said to them, "Don't be afraid."

(Hold up the "sea in a bottle." Slightly tilt it from one side to the other to create waves. Then tip it farther to make bigger waves to show a violent storm. Watch the piece of foil to see how high the waves are and how difficult it would be to walk on the water during a storm.) One of the disciples, Peter, said, "If it's really you, let me walk on the water to you." Jesus told him to come. As he climbed out of the boat, Peter was amazed that he wasn't sinking in the water. Keeping his eyes on Jesus, Peter walked toward Him. Suddenly he was distracted and took his eyes off Jesus. He started to sink, but Jesus rescued him from the waves.

Isn't it interesting that when Peter kept his eyes on Jesus and trusted Him, he was able to walk on the water. As soon as Peter looked away, he started to sink. You know, that's the way it is with us. If we keep our minds on Jesus and trust Him, He will help us. When other things become more important and we look to them instead of Jesus, we start having trouble. When we need courage to face a frightening situation, we can look to Jesus and He will provide the courage we need.

by Vicki Totel

0-382-30647-3

GOD'S LOVE FOR ME
John 3:16

When I want to learn more about something, I look it up in a dictionary, an encyclopedia, or a book in the library. When I want to know something about God, I look it up in my Bible. My Bible is a kind of reference book where I find out about God's love for me.

(Read John 3:16.) This is the Bible verse I most often think of when someone mentions the love of God. I like it because I can put my name in place of the words "the world" and make it really special to me. (Read the verse again with your name in it.) No matter how many people there are in the world—in 1990 the world population was about 5,288,000,000 (I looked that up in an encyclopedia.)—God loves me!

I also read in my Bible about God's love in Jeremiah 31:3. (Read it aloud.) My dictionary says that *everlasting* means "never coming to an end." A lot of things I know have an end: the books I read end, my favorite candy bar ends much too soon, and the day ends too. God will love me forever. His love will never end.

(Read 1 John 3:1.) My dictionary says that *lavished* means "being very generous." I don't have to look very far to see how generous God is to me. I know that Jesus loves me. I have a wonderful family, friends, teachers, church family (make this statement personal). How about you? How do you know God loves you? (Encourage children to share as they feel comfortable.) Remember to look in your Bible to find out how much God loves you.

by Karen Berger

0-382-30647-3

THE GOLDEN RULE
Matthew 7:7-12

Materials Needed: Several types of measuring rulers

Growing up can be measured in several ways. Do you know how long you were when you were born? Do you know the newborn length of a younger brother or sister? (Most babies are 18"-21" at birth. Wait for children's responses. Then measure some of them to see how tall they are now. Comment on how much they have grown.)

You can also tell how much you are growing by the things you can do now that you couldn't do when you were younger. Someone used to feed you. Now you can do that yourself! Can you think of other things you can do? (Catch a ball, build with blocks, write your name, etc.)

There is another way to tell you are growing. You are growing up to be in charge of your own behavior. Right now you have many people to help you with growing up inside–parents, teachers, friends, your church family. But sometimes you need to learn to be in charge of your actions for yourself.

The Bible gives you a ruler to measure yourself for growing inside. (Read Matthew 7:12.) You should treat other people as you want them to treat you. Be kind–let someone else be first in line. Be loving–help someone who spilled a glass of milk. What are other ways you can treat others as you want them to treat you? (Wait for responses. Suggest some such as waiting to be called on for an answer, not always blurting the answer out before everyone else.)

Use God's Golden Rule to guide you and measure your growth as a Christian.

by Karen Berger

GROWING AS A CHRISTIAN
1 Peter 2:2

Materials Needed: Several pictures of a child, ranging in age from newborn to about ten years (You want to show the process of growth, so all the pictures should be of the same child. The pictures should be as large as possible.)

I brought some pictures to show you today, boys and girls. Do you like to look at pictures? The first one is of a baby, a brand new person just starting life. He can't really do much except lie down. He can't even turn over by himself. This picture is of the same baby, a little bit older and bigger, but still not able to do much for himself. In this next picture we can see the baby is big enough to sit up alone now. In this one, he can stand up. He probably can eat by himself now. Here's a picture where he is much 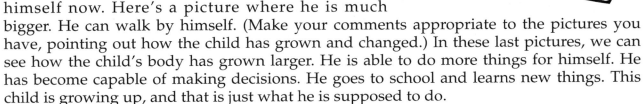 bigger. He can walk by himself. (Make your comments appropriate to the pictures you have, pointing out how the child has grown and changed.) In these last pictures, we can see how the child's body has grown larger. He is able to do more things for himself. He has become capable of making decisions. He goes to school and learns new things. This child is growing up, and that is just what he is supposed to do.

When he was born, this child's parents knew he was pretty helpless. They knew they had to take care of him and teach him how to do things. They knew he could drink only milk or baby formula. He wasn't ready for cheeseburgers or pizza. But they expected him to grow up someday. If he hadn't grown, they would have been very worried about him.

When I first became a Christian, I was like this first picture–a little baby who couldn't do much by myself. (Hold up first picture again.) I had to learn basic things about being a Christian and about God, like a baby who drinks only milk and can't even sit up or crawl. After I spent time reading my Bible and coming to church to learn more about God and how He wants me to live, I grew a little bit stronger. (Hold up slightly older baby picture.) I was growing spiritually like a child grows physically. I became better at living the way God wants me to live, as I learned more about Jesus. (Flip through the rest of the pictures as you talk about growth.)

God knows that each of us is like a baby when we first come into His family. The Bible tells us to start with the basic things in the Bible and keep growing. So remember to stay close to God, read your Bible, and pray every day. Don't get discouraged if you find yourself falling back into old habits. Remember how many times a baby falls when he is learning to walk. Just ask God for forgiveness and start living for Him again. All of us can learn more about God, no matter how old we are. We all start like this (show newborn picture) and we want to grow to this (show oldest picture) and even further. We never stop growing in our Christian lives. (Read 1 Peter 2:2.)

by Carolyn Larsen

0-382-30647-3

HAPPINESS
Matthew 5:1-12

Materials Needed: A broken, obviously discarded toy or game

What did you want last year for your birthday? What did you think would make you really happy? (Unless the children have recently had birthdays, they may not remember.) What did you want for a Christmas present last year—what was the one thing that would make you happy for the holidays? (Wait for several children to share responses.) Sometimes we think there is only one thing that can really make us happy. But if we can't even remember what we wanted last year, how happy did it really make us? And did that happiness last?

(Show the broken toy or game.) Did this ever happen to the thing you thought you really wanted to make you happy? (Give children a chance to share their experiences.) Somehow you were disappointed with the thing you thought you wanted. It just didn't measure up to what you thought it would be. It didn't bring you the happiness you wanted from it.

Sometimes people think the only way to be happy is by having lots of things. Then when those things disappoint them, they become unhappy. Jesus taught His disciples that there are many ways to have happiness. Those who want to do right more than anything else and those who work to bring peace are happy people. Jesus was teaching us that to be happy we need to be doing right. Jesus did not say that buying something for fun or receiving a present was wrong. But He wants us to know that **true** happiness comes from loving Him and sharing His love with others.

by Karen Berger

0-382-30647-3

HELPING OTHERS
1 Thessalonians 5:14b

Done

When do you need help? Do people help you? Do you ever help others with things that are hard for them? How do you help around the house? (Wait for several children to respond.)

The first day of school! How exciting! Best friends Kimberly and Megan could hardly wait to meet their teacher. As the bell rang, the noisy children entered the school. The girls saw that some of their favorite friends were in their class.

As the class quieted to start playing a game, Kim noticed that Michael was in their class too. She always liked Michael. He was a very kind boy, quite smart, and confined to a wheelchair. It always made Kim feel good inside when she could help Michael. He needed help from the whole class since basic things most of them did easily were difficult for Michael.

As the school year passed, it was a little harder than Kim had thought. She was kind of concerned because she was having a hard time with reading. Some of those words seemed too hard! She wondered if she should ask for help.

After the report cards came out, her mom agreed with the teacher that Kim needed a little help. She decided that Michael and Kim should be teamed up together, since Michael was such a good reader.

As the year went by Kim and Michael became good friends. Kim improved in her reading and even started to like it a bit. One day Michael told Kim that being able to help her made him feel good. He said, "Usually people are so busy helping me because of my disability, I don't ever get a chance to help someone else. I like it. It makes me feel like I'm important if I can help."

God wants us to help others. Jesus spent His whole life helping people. Are you following His example? (Read 1 Thessalonians 5:14b.)

by Vicki Totel

Shining Star, Copyright © 1995

0-382-30647-3

IMITATING JESUS
Ephesians 5:1

Do you know how to play the game "Simon Says"? Would you like to play it with me? I will do something and if I say, "Simon says do this," then you do it. If I don't say, "Simon says," then don't do it.

OK, everyone stand up. Uh, oh, some of you stood up, but Simon didn't say to stand up, did he? Simon says hop on one foot. (Hop with the children.) Simon says stop. Stretch your hands up high. (If you catch some kids doing this, point it out.) Simon says jump up and down. (Jump with the kids.) Simon says run in place. (Do so.) Sit down. Aahh, I caught a few of you with that one. Simon didn't say to sit down. You must be careful to imitate only the things that Simon says.

It's fun to copy other peoples' actions sometimes, isn't it? In fact, copying or imitating others is one way we learn the right way to live. Small children copy their parents to learn how to do chores around the house such as cleaning the floors or washing dishes or folding laundry.

We can also copy someone else to learn how to treat other people, but it is important to copy the right person. Who do you think would be the best person to copy? I think a good example for any of us to imitate would be Jesus.

Let's think of how Jesus lived and some ways He treated others. (Ask children to mention some of Jesus' characteristics.) He was loving, kind, gentle, and patient. He prayed often, helped others, and put others' needs before His own. Those are all good things to copy. We would be nice people and Jesus would be pleased with us if we did those things.

We are told in the Bible that we should imitate God, like children imitate their parents. (Read Ephesians 5:1.) Why don't you choose one characteristic of Jesus today and imitate it every chance you get. If you ask Him, God will help you become more like Jesus every day.

by Carolyn Larsen

JESUS WAS A CHILD TOO
Luke 2:41-51

Do you ever have a hard time thinking of Jesus as a little boy? Do you wonder what kind of games He played or how He looked when He lost His first tooth or if He willingly helped with His chores around the house?

When Jesus was twelve years old, He and His family went to Jerusalem for the Passover Feast. Friends and relatives traveled together in a large group from their home in Nazareth to Jerusalem and back again. As they walked along the roads, the women and children walked at the front of the group and the men towards the back to protect everyone. Since Jesus was twelve, He probably could have been in either group. On the trip home His mother Mary probably thought He was with Joseph, and Joseph assumed He was with Mary. At the end of the day, Mary and Joseph realized that Jesus was missing and was nowhere in the large group of travelers. They were frightened and worried, wondering what had happened to Him. They returned to Jerusalem, retracing their steps to try to find Him.

After looking for Jesus for three days, they finally found Him in the temple. He had been so interested in a discussion with the religious leaders in the temple, He had stayed behind instead of heading back to Nazareth with His parents. Jesus had been eager to listen and to ask questions of the teachers who had been in the temple for the feast. The teachers were amazed by His wisdom and His intelligent questions.

Jesus knew that His purpose on earth was to "be about His Father's business," which meant that He needed to do what God wanted Him to do. (Luke 2:49, KJV) His time in the temple was only the beginning of His work on earth.

God wants each of us to "be about our Father's business." That means we should be obeying God's Word and sharing His love with others. Even when Jesus was a child, He lived for the Lord. So can you.

by Vicki Totel

KINDNESS
1 Thessalonians 5:15

Materials Needed: A piece of string or yarn to tie around your finger and a piece for each child

(Show the children your finger with the string tied around it.) Do you know what this string is for? Did you know there are Bible verses that tell the real value of tying a string around my finger? (Read Deuteronomy 6:1-9 or say it in your own words.)

Sometimes it's a good idea to remind ourselves of what we are doing or what needs to be done. We can do the same thing with our manners, especially our "kindness" manners. Manners are how we act or behave. How can we always remember to be kind and have good manners? We should try to leave every place and person better than we found them. Help me think of some ways we could do that. (Discuss ideas such as picking up litter when we see it, cleaning the table when our meal is over, saying kind words to people, thanking people for helping us, hugging people to show that we love them.)

Let me give you some string to help you remember to be kind and helpful today. I'll begin by helping you tie the string on your finger!

by Karen Berger

KNOWING WHAT TO BELIEVE
2 Timothy 3:16

Materials Needed: Make several signs with confusing messages such as: Up Is Down; To Go Right, Turn Left; Stand Only in the Sitting Area; In Is Out

(Display the signs.) My goodness, aren't these signs confusing? If I were trying to read them to figure out which way to go or what to do, I would have a hard time.

Have you ever gone on a long car trip with your parents? How do you get ready for the trip? You may pack the car full of suitcases and pillows and snack food and things to do while you travel. Then Dad or Mom takes out the road map and decides which roads you need to take in order to get where you want to go.

What would happen if you were driving along on your trip, following the roads outlined on the map, when suddenly the road didn't go where the map said it should go? Let's imagine that after driving in circles for a while, your dad stops in a small town at a little grocery store to ask for directions. There are two old men sitting on the front porch of the grocery store. When your dad asks them for help, they both gladly give directions, but they don't agree. One says, go this way (point left) but the other says, go this way (point right). Dad comes back to the car totally confused. How do you know which of these nice old men to believe?

There really isn't any way to know which one is right, until you test what they have told you. Sometimes it is hard to know what is the right thing to believe because it is hard to know whom to trust.

I know someone you can always trust–God. Whatever He says is absolutely true. But where do you find out what God has to say to you? (Wait for children's ideas.) You look in the Bible. The Bible is God's Word to His people, a road map for the right way to live. (Read 2 Timothy 3:16.) The words in the Bible come from God. He gave us the Bible so we will know how to live.

You know that when you read the Bible, you can believe it because it is God's Word. If someone tells you that it is OK for you to do something which you aren't sure about, read the Bible too and find out what is right and wrong. Just remember, when things around you are confusing, look at the Bible, God's road map for you.

by Carolyn Larsen

Shining Star, Copyright © 1995
0-382-30647-3

THE LIGHT OF THE WORLD
Matthew 5:14-16

Materials Needed: A magic birthday cake candle that relights when it is blown out (test it beforehand to be sure it relights), a match, a glass of water to put the candle out

Did you know that other people can see what Jesus is like by watching how Christians live? We are like advertisements for Jesus. (Read Matthew 5:14.) Jesus' love inside us is like a light shining in a dark night. (Light the candle and hold it up.) Other people can look at us and see what Jesus' love is like by the way we show it to others. They can watch how we treat other people and how we handle disappointments or anger. Does Jesus' love show in your life?

It's hard to always be a good example, isn't it? Sometimes we may be tired and certainly don't feel like shining. (Blow candle out.) When we are tired or grumpy, it is easier to just not have anyone know we are Christians. We may even feel like our lights have gone out during those times. (Candle relights.) Oh, the light is back. The light wasn't *really* out, and Jesus' love inside you doesn't go away when you are tired or grumpy either.

When you get in trouble with Mom and Dad and they are angry with you and send you to your room, does your light go out? (Blow candle out.) Does Jesus' love go away when you are angry? (Candle relights.) Well, what's this? The light is back. Yes, Jesus' love is always there inside you, no matter what happens, just waiting for you to let it shine.

Jesus' love for you never goes away. He loves you no matter what. Bad things that happen to you may temporarily cover up the light of His love, so it may seem like it has gone out. But it hasn't.

Remember, you are the light of the world. Other people can see what Jesus is like by watching you. Be careful to let His love show through you. Let Him help you through hard times, disappointments, or even when you are tired and grumpy. Be careful to never cover up His light; let it shine for all to see. (If time permits, lead children in singing "This Little Light of Mine.")

by Carolyn Larsen

THE LORD IS MY SHEPHERD
Psalm 23

Cori was about to start a new grade in school. It was in a bigger building than where she had gone before. There would be many more students and a different schedule. She was pretty nervous about it.

On the first day of school, she slowly walked into the new school building. She wasn't even sure where to go once she was in the building. She was afraid she would be late for class. Hundreds of students rushed around her as she stood in the main hallway. No one paid any attention to the lonely girl standing by herself.

Then a girl named Sara came hurrying through the hall. Sara knew her way around the school building. She had seen Cori at church, and now she could see that Cori was nervous. So she offered to help. "Hey Cori," she called across the hallway. Cori was certainly glad to see a familiar face from church. "Where are you supposed to go?" Sara asked.

Cori told her the room number and Sara said, "Come on, I'll show you where it is." Sara led her through the building to her classroom.

Sara did this all day. She would appear, almost as if by magic, at the end of every class period and would help Cori find the room for her next class. By the end of the day, Cori knew her way around the school building. She had even met some new friends through Sara. Sara's guidance and help made that first day of school much easier for Cori.

Sara acted as a shepherd or guide for Cori. The Lord is like a shepherd for us. In John 10, Jesus says He is our Good Shepherd. What does a shepherd do for his sheep? He guides them to food and water. He protects them from danger. He leads them and helps them any way he can. Jesus will guide us through life if we let Him. He will make sure we have all we need to be healthy and strong. He will protect us from the bad things that could hurt us. When we give our lives over to Him, our Good Shepherd stays with us to lovingly help us find our way.

by Carolyn Larsen

Shining Star, Copyright © 1995

0-382-30647-3

THE NAME OF JESUS
Matthew 1:18-25

Materials Needed: A book of names with their meanings

(Share with the children what your name is, what it means, and how you received your name. Then ask the children their names and if they know the "story" of their names. You might want to look up a few names in the book of names and be ready to share their meanings.) Some parents know what they are going to name their children even before their children are born. Some parents select both a boy's name and a girl's name before the birth of their child so they are ready no matter what. Some choose to wait to decide on a name until after their child is born. Some parents choose a name just because they like the name. Others name their child after a relative or friend. Some choose a name they have heard and liked or read in a story.

An angel told Joseph and Mary what to name the child Mary was expecting. The angel said that Mary would give birth to a Son, and they were to give Him the name Jesus because Jesus would save His people from their sins. The name *Jesus* means "Savior," the One who would save people. Jesus had several other names. Two of them were *Christ* and *Messiah* which mean "chosen one." When used together, Jesus Christ, this means that Jesus was chosen by God to save people from their sins.

Our names are often the very first gifts given to us by our parents, those who love us. Jesus' name is a real gift to us too. It reminds us of how much He loves us and of what He did for us. What a special name! It should remind us to thank God for sending His Son to earth for us.

by Karen Berger

0-382-30647-3

OBEDIENCE
1 John 5:1-5

Materials Needed: A recipe book, a package of garden seeds with directions on it, an instruction manual for an appliance, a driver's license manual, or something else that gives instructions

In everything we do, there are rules to be followed. If we are going to make cookies, we follow the rules of the recipe. (Hold up recipe book.) If we are going to plant a garden, we follow the rules of gardening. (Hold up seed package.) If we are going to use a VCR, we follow the rules for its operating instructions. (Hold up instruction manual.) If we are going to drive a car, we need to follow the rules of the road. (Hold up driver's manual.) Rules help us when we obey them.

Even in nature there are rules. How else does the caterpillar know when to spin its cocoon or when to break the cocoon and spread its wings and fly? How else would a bear know when to hibernate in the winter or wake up in the spring?

Can any of you share an experience when you or someone you know forgot to follow the rules? (Suggestions might include the following: forgetting to put the sugar in the cookies, planting the bean seeds too deep, forgetting to plug in the VCR, or not stopping at the red light.) That's when things go wrong, when we don't follow the rules. That's also what happens when we don't follow God's rules. (Read 1 John 5:1-5.) Jesus said the greatest commandment is to love God with all our heart, soul, and mind. And the second one is to love our neighbors as we love ourselves. If we follow these two rules, we will show God how much we love Him, and our lives will be what He wants them to be.

by Karen Berger

0-382-30647-3

THE CHURCH
1 Corinthians 12:12-27

(Call on specific children in your group.) Susan, what is the most important part of your body? James, what is the most important part of your body? How about you David? (Let children say what they think. Agree with them; each part they mention is a very important part.)

Each part of your body is very important and has a purpose. Your baby toe may not seem all that important, but if you stub your toe, ouch, you really feel the hurt! I don't think too often of my elbow, but if it gets bumped, I'm very aware of it. On the other hand, my ears are very important. I use them all the time, but I don't really think about them until I get an ear infection. God made the parts of our bodies so they would work together and be useful. One part of your body is not more important than another part.

If one of your eyes is not happy being an eye and decides it would rather be a leg, you would be in big trouble! If your ear gets tired of hearing all the time and decides it would rather be a hand, how would you hear? Your head cannot say to your feet, "I really don't need you anymore. You're not as important as I am." Your knees cannot say to your shoulders, "I'm much better than you are. I don't need you on my back anymore." All the parts of your body are necessary and fit together to work properly.

That's the way the church is. (Read 1 Corinthians 12:12-27.) The church is like a body. Each of us in the church needs the others. The choir cannot say to the Sunday School teachers, "You are not as important as I am. We don't need you anymore." The ushers cannot say to the pastor, "We don't need you anymore because we are more important." Each part of the church needs the other part so we can all work together. We need pastors, teachers, nursery workers, adults, and children, just as our bodies need eyes, ears, hands, and feet. One part is not more important than the other part. God made all parts of our bodies so they could work together. The church needs to work together as one body as well.

What do you think you can do to help your church? Talk about it with your parents today.

by Vicki Totel

PALM SUNDAY PARADE
Matthew 21:1-11

Materials Needed: A large palm branch

Do you like parades? I sure do. I go downtown on the Fourth of July and take my lawn chair, my camera, a thermos of ice water, some donut holes, and a little American flag to wave. I get there early so I can set my chair right on the curb and have a good view of everything. Pretty soon the sidewalk and sides of the street are filled with people waiting for the parade to begin. We all smile at each other and enjoy being together, even though we don't know each other.

Pretty soon we hear cheering and music way off down the street, and we know the parade has started. Before long, the first band and float have come by and it's wonderful! I stand up every time an American flag is carried by, and I cheer for the bands and laugh at the clowns. It's great. I love to watch a parade.

You know, Jesus was once in a parade, but He was the only person in the parade. Jesus rode into Jerusalem on a donkey that His disciples had borrowed for Him. You may be wondering how it could be a parade with only one person in it. People had heard about all the miracles Jesus had done. They had heard all the wonderful things He taught about God. So many, many people came to see Jesus ride by. They took off their coats and laid them in the street for Him to ride over. They cut branches like this one off palm trees and laid them on the street for His donkey to walk on. Some people waved the palm branches above Him as He passed. (Wave your palm branch.) They shouted, "Hosanna to the Son of David! Blessed is He who comes in the name of the Lord! Hosanna in the highest!" You see, they thought Jesus was a king. He **is** our heavenly king, but they thought He was going to become the king of their nation.

It was some parade! Everyone in the whole city of Jerusalem wanted to know who the man on the donkey was. The simple answer was, "He is Jesus, the prophet from Nazareth." We know that Jesus was more than a prophet though. He was the Son of God!

Jesus let the crowds cheer for Him. He accepted all the attention of the people. But He knew what was going to happen to Him in Jerusalem. He knew that He would be arrested and would die. But He rode into the city anyway. He was willing to go through all that because He loved those people watching Him go by, and He loves us, you and me. That is why Palm Sunday is a very special day. It's a reminder of everything Jesus was willing to do for us and of how much He cares for you and for me.

by Carolyn Larsen

Shining Star, Copyright © 1995
0-382-30647-3

PRAYER
Matthew 6:5-15

There are times during our worship services, family devotions or even when we are by ourselves that we want to say a quiet prayer. Sometimes we may forget how to pray or what to pray for. I'll tell you how you can use your hand to always remind you how to pray and what to pray about.

Your thumb can remind you of how thankful you should always be. (Hold up your thumb.) What are you thankful for? Try to look for a reason to be thankful for everything that happens to you.

We often use our index finger for pointing. Let's use it to remind us to pray for those who point "the way" for us. (Hold up index finger with thumb.) Do you pray for your teachers and church leaders? Do you pray for the leaders of our country?

Your tall finger can remind you to pray for your family because they have a "tall" part in your life. (Hold up third finger along with thumb and index finger.) The tall finger can remind you to pray for dads and moms, brothers and sisters, grandparents, aunts and uncles, and even your pets!

The fourth finger is sometimes called your "weak" finger. (Hold up fourth finger with others and wiggle it.) If you have played the piano or another musical instrument, you know that this is the finger which is the most difficult to train. It doesn't have much strength. It can remind you to pray for people you know who are sick, needy and hungry people, and for anyone who has a problem.

Your last finger, your "pinky", can help you remember to pray for yourself. You have private things you want to talk to God about, or you may want to ask God for help with something.

Try to pray through all the fingers on your hand each time you pray. You may want to begin with a different finger each time. You'll always have a "handy" reminder for prayer right there on the end of your arm.

by Karen Berger

0-382-30647-3

PREJUDICE
James 2:1-14

Materials Needed: Remove the labels from several cans (You may want to mark them for your own use later on!)

(Show the children the unlabeled cans.) Can anyone tell me what is in this can? (Hold up a can and let the children make several guesses.) But how can we tell for sure? (Encourage the children to make suggestions such as opening the cans, X-raying the cans, comparing them to similar cans.) All of this wouldn't be necessary if we could read the labels, would it?

Do you ever "label" anything else before you really know what is inside? (Wait for responses.)

What about people such as other boys and girls? When you have a new classmate in school or Sunday School, do you think you already know what the person is like because you have seen his or her label (clothes, hair, color of skin)? Or do you wait until you have spent some time with that person before you decide what they're like inside?

(Read James 2:1-14.) The rich man's dress and jewelry was his "label." There was nothing wrong with the rich man dressing this way, but people in the church were not supposed to show favoritism. They were supposed to love their neighbors. God says we should not be prejudiced. We should not just look at the way people appear on the outside to decide if we like them. Don't just look at labels! Be sure you know what is inside. You might miss something you would really like!

by Karen Berger

0-382-30647-3

SATAN
Hebrews 4:15-16

Materials Needed: A long stick with a long string on the end with a carrot tied to the string and a big bag of carrots

Do you know who Satan is? Did you know that he used to be an angel in heaven? He had to leave heaven when he sinned by deciding that he was more important than God. God doesn't allow sin in heaven. Now Satan tries to keep all of us from knowing and obeying God. How can Satan keep us away from God? He gets us sidetracked from learning about God or trying to live like Jesus. (Take out the stick with a carrot on it.) This stick with a carrot on it is a way people used to try to get their donkeys to go where they wanted. A donkey wanted to eat the carrot, so he walked toward it. It was always a few steps ahead of him, so he kept walking toward it.

You might be going through life doing just fine. You may read your Bible every day and talk to God every day. You may be learning to live like Jesus, being kind and considerate and loving. Then Satan dangles something in front of you. (Hold stick up high, so carrot dangles in front of children.) Of course, it won't be a carrot. Maybe it's popularity. He makes it look like if you are willing to go along with the crowd and do some things that aren't really right, then you'll be popular with everyone.

Maybe Satan tempts you with stealing. You have a chance to pick up a video game in a store or at a friend's house and slip it in your pocket. No one would know, and you would have a terrific game!

He may get you with something as simple as a TV show. He might tempt you to watch a show that is on late at night. When its over, you are too tired to read your Bible and talk to God. That way, Satan pulls you away from God.

It's hard to fight the things that Satan holds in front of you. They always look so good. They are always things you would like. They might not even be bad by themselves. But if these things pull you away from God and living for Him, then Satan has won. He has done what he set out to do. You may get the thing he tempts you with. (Take carrot off.) But Satan always has something new to hold in front of you the next time. (Hold up whole bag of carrots.) He never runs out of ways to try to keep you away from God.

How can you fight against Satan's temptations? Talk to the Lord about it. Satan tempted Jesus too, but Jesus never gave in. He understands how you feel when you are tempted. He wants to help you resist Satan. (Read Hebrews 4:15-16.) Be strong in your efforts to read the Bible every day, talk to God every day. Fight Satan and push him away. Keep God number one in your life.

by Carolyn Larsen

Shining Star, Copyright © 1995

0-382-30647-3

SHARING WHAT GOD GIVES ME
Hebrews 13:16

Materials Needed: A big candy bar (or other treat), enough small pieces of candy (or other treat) for each child

(If you're using another kind of treat, adapt the following comments.) Hey everyone, look what I have! (Hold up big candy bar. Be very excited about this.) I was just walking in here and someone came up to me and just gave me this candy bar, for free. She just gave it to me and said, "Here, I want you to have this." Can you believe it? I love candy bars, especially big chocolately ones like this. (Begin to open the wrapper.) I just love to settle down with a good chocolate bar and my favorite book. (Take a bite.) Ummm, is this good! (If any of the children ask for some of the candy, just ignore them. Be absorbed in your candy. Take several bites.) You know, I think this tastes even better than usual because it was free. I really did nothing to deserve it.

(Suddenly notice children sitting there, as you are licking your fingers.) Oh dear, I should have been sharing this with you, shouldn't I? That would have been the nice thing to do, wouldn't it? (Take another bite.) I mean, I did get the candy bar for free.

I feel bad, but you know, this is a good reminder to share all that God has given me. God has given each of us so much. We should be sharing with those around us every chance we get. There may be someone who needs clothing, and I have extra sweatshirts. Maybe another person needs food; I can share mine. There may be a child who needs toys, and I sure have more than I need. There may even be someone who needs a Bible, and I have more than one, so I can give one away.

God has given us talents we can share too. Some people can sing, some can write, some can draw pictures, some can sew clothes or curtains. All of us have talents we can share with others.

Remember that everything you have, your clothes and food and even your talents of singing or playing an instrument, are all gifts from God. He is pleased when you share your possessions and talents with others. (Read Hebrews 13:16.)

Now, I have a small reminder for each of you. It will help you remember to share everything God has given you. I didn't share my big candy bar with you and I'm really sorry, but I do have some candy for each of you. As you enjoy it, think about what you have that you could share with others.

by Carolyn Larsen

0-382-30647-3

SIN
1 John 1:8-10

Materials Needed: A variety of strong smelling items

I have something for you to smell today. (Depending on your group and the time available, let them smell various items. You may want to have them close their eyes and try to guess the items you have by their smells: for example, fresh baked cookies or muffins, perfume or shaving lotion, flower, new sneakers, vinegar.)

Don't you just love to smell the grass after it has been cut? How about a crackling fire in the fireplace on a cold night? What is your favorite smell? God gave us the sense of smell to help us enjoy many things. I have a true story for you today about a different smell.

One night, Vicki was dog-sitting for a friend. Toto, the tiny dog she was keeping, was sitting at her feet in the doorway of the garage. They were enjoying the sweet smell of fresh rain on the grass. In a flash, Toto jumped to her feet and ran to the edge of the grass, investigating what Vicki thought must be a bug that had peaked her interest. An instant later, in the dark Vicki saw two small white streaks and Toto, with panic in her eyes, jumping at her. A horrible smell filled the air. Toto had been sprayed by a skunk! Have you ever smelled a skunk? It is a smell you will never forget and it **does not** go away.

Toto ran into the house and started rubbing her head on the rug. Poor dog! She was so frightened she didn't know what to do! Vicki didn't want the smell of skunk in her house, so she picked up the dog and took her outside again. After a bath of tomato juice (which is supposed to be the only thing to get rid of the skunk smell), Toto was wrapped in towels to keep her from shaking herself and splattering tomato all over. Toto was shivering and still quite smelly, although she seemed to enjoy licking the tomato juice off her fur!

You know, that smell of skunk is a lot like sin. We don't really plan on sinning any more than Toto planned to meet a skunk. But suddenly, we've done something wrong. There are many kinds of sin: cheating, stealing, lying, and anything we do that does not please God and breaks His rules for living. We all sin because we were born in sin and live in a sinful world.

Our sin is the reason Jesus came into this world, so He could take the punishment for our sin. (Read 1 John 1:8-10.)

The only thing that will take care of your sin is confessing it to Jesus, telling Him you have done wrong. He will forgive you. Just like Toto had to have a tomato juice bath to take care of her smell, we need to be cleansed of our sin by Jesus. Tomato juice didn't completely get rid of Toto's smell, but Jesus' forgiveness gets rid of our sin without a trace. Aren't you glad we don't have to smell like sin?

by Vicki Totel

0-382-30647-3

STAYING HEALTHY INSIDE AND OUTSIDE
John 6:35

What is your favorite food? (Wait for response.) If you could have anything to eat, what would you eat? How often would you eat it?

Wouldn't it be fun, when you wake up in the morning and stumble out to the table, to be greeted with a large plate of donuts and soda pop to drink? Sounds yummy, doesn't it? Then when the lunch bell rings at school, you could grab your lunchbox and enjoy a large bag of chips, some candy bars, and another soda pop. Hey, this is living! After a long afternoon at school, you go home to a large piece of chocolate cake and four more candy bars. By then your stomach might feel just a little funny and your teeth might hurt a bit, but it tastes so good! For dinner your Mom lets you have candy-coated peanuts, a sugar-flavored drink, caramel corn, licorice (both red and black), and ice cream. As you settle down to homework that evening, you have a plate of chocolate chip cookies. MMMMM! Isn't this wonderful. At bedtime, instead of brushing your teeth, your Mom let's you have a jawbreaker! Wouldn't that be great? (Let children respond.)

Guess what, the next day when you wake up, you might not feel too well. You might have a stomachache. Why? Sweets and junk food aren't what we need to make us healthy.

What kind of food do we need to have for healthy bodies? (Let children suggest some things.) Our bodies need a balanced diet: fruits and vegetables, breads and cereal, meat, and milk. These foods help us grow. They give us strong bones and muscles and healthy teeth, hair, and skin. There are many varieties of foods we can eat. We can even eat sweets sometimes, but not all the time. God made our bodies so that we get energy and nutrition from various kinds of foods.

There is something else we need to be healthy. We need to provide nutrition for our spiritual needs, for the inside part of us. (Read John 6:35.) Does that mean that if you believe in Jesus, you will never have to eat again because you will never be hungry? You'll never be thirsty for a drink? No, what it means is that your soul will be fed. Just like our bodies need bread to be healthy and strong, our souls need the Bread of Life, Jesus, to be happy and healthy on the inside.

Sometimes we look for other things to take the place of Jesus in our lives. Sometimes we think a nice home or new toys would be good for us. Maybe getting good grades, winning a sports tournament, or having lots of friends would really make us happy. These things would make us feel good for awhile, but they don't last. Jesus gives us happiness, spiritual health, that lasts forever. A steady diet of Bible reading and prayer and learning about Jesus at church will keep us healthy on the inside!

by Vicki Totel

Shining Star, Copyright © 1995

0-382-30647-3

TAMING THE TONGUE
James 3:1-9

Materials Needed: A picture of a cowboy on a horse and a picture of a ship with a rudder

Let me see your tongue. (Encourage students to stick their tongues out as far as they can.) What do you do with your tongue? (Wait for responses.) Tongues are very useful, aren't they? They help us taste whether something is sweet or sour. They help us swallow our food. They really get a lot of use when we talk. They help us form words and sounds. Tongues help us whistle! Tongues help us get the peanut butter off the roof of our mouths. They really are handy things to have!

Do you know how a cowboy controls where his horse is to go? (Hold up picture and wait for responses.) There is a little piece of metal called a bit that fits into a horse's mouth. The bit is attached to the reins a cowboy holds. When he wants to go right, he pulls the reins to the right, a signal to the horse that he should turn that way. Even though the bit is very small compared to the size of the horse, it can control a big horse.

The same is true about a little rudder on a big ship. (Hold up picture. Point out rudder.) Even though the winds are blowing, a ship can be controlled and given direction by this little rudder. Think for a moment about the difference in size between a rudder and a big ship and between a bit and a large horse. Now think of the difference between the size of your little tongue and the rest of your body.

The Bible says that your tongue is a small part of your body, but it can make or break you. (Read James 3:1-9.) Our little innocent-looking tongues can be used to praise God and encourage those around us. It can also be used to complain and say hateful things about people. The writer of the book of James says, "Out of the same mouth come praise and cursing." People can tame all kinds of wild animals, but we still have a hard time making our tongues behave.

Let's try to be very careful in the way we use our tongues. Let's ask God every day to help us say only words that are helpful, not harmful.

by Vicki Totel

0-382-30647-3

TREATING MY BODY RIGHT
I Corinthians 3:16

Materials Needed: A bottle of bubbles which has been emptied and refilled with plain water (Keep the bubble blower in the bottle.)

What is this I have here? Right, it's a bottle of bubbles. It's fun to blow bubbles and watch them float through the air. I like to try to catch the bubbles before they burst on the ground. Shall I blow a few bubbles right now? (Open the bottle and make several attempts to blow some bubbles.)

I'm not getting any bubbles. I don't understand what's wrong. Let me check the bottle. (Read the label.) Yes, this is a bottle of bubbles. I should be able to just dip the wand in and gently blow some bubbles. (Try again.) Well, it still isn't working. I'm really sorry. (Dip finger in bubble liquid and taste it.) Here's the problem. This isn't bubble liquid at all; it's just plain water. I certainly can't blow bubbles with plain water. You know what I think happened? Someone put the wrong thing in this bottle, and now it can't do what it is supposed to do.

You know what this reminds me of? Our bodies. If we don't put the right things in our bodies, they can't do what they are supposed to do. Your body should be growing stronger and healthier every year so you can run and play and learn new things. But in order for you to be able to do that, you need to be filling your body with vegetables and fruits and milk and other healthy foods. Filling your body with drugs or alcohol will keep you from growing strong and healthy. Then your body will not be able to do the things it is supposed to do for you. (Read 1 Corinthians 3:16.)

Your body is God's temple, the place where God lives. It's your responsibility to treat God's home right and make it a good place for Him to live. That means you should be filling it with the right kinds of food, drink, exercising, and getting enough rest. Then your body will be strong and healthy so that you can use it to serve God and do the work He wants you to do.

by Carolyn Larsen

0-382-30647-3

WE BELONG TO EACH OTHER
Romans 12:1-8

Materials Needed: A magnet and several large and small paper clips (If possible include some plastic-coated ones.)

As I look around our church I see many different kinds of people. There are some older people, some younger, and some children. There are tall people, short people, skinny people and some not-so-skinny ones. Some are very musical while others can't sing but are great at basketball. Some like to read, some like to talk, some are good at building things, and some like to paint pictures. Some are good at telling stories and some are good at explaining what the Bible means. Some people are good at keeping the church building clean, some are good at running the sound equipment, and some are good at playing the organ or piano.

We are all very different aren't we? We don't all have the same abilities or even the same interests. I wonder why we all ended up here in this church? I wonder why there aren't churches that are full of just musicians? Or why isn't there a church of just great cooks? Or just good teachers? I'm happy that churches are not divided that way, aren't you? I would miss the good things we have here in our church because we are all so different with different talents.

You know, this is the way God planned for churches to be. (Read Romans 12:1-8.) Each of us has a different job to do in the church in order for our church to be the best it can be. We belong to each other and we each need the other people here.

But what is it that holds us all together? There is some power that makes all the different interests and talents stick together. Do you see what I have here? It is a magnet and some paper clips. Some of the paper clips are big, some are small, some are white, some are pink. Look what happens when the magnet gets near these paper clips. They all jump right onto the magnet. They are connected to each other because of the power of the magnet.

We are connected to each other here in our church because of the power of God. His love is so mighty that it holds us all together. We belong to Him, so we belong to each other too. People who don't have a whole lot in common are brought together and held together because of their love for God and His love for them. Isn't that great?

Aren't you glad to be part of this church, held together by God's love? Each one of us has a job to do in order for our church to be the best that it can be for God. So look around. Every person you see is important to the church and so are you! Let's appreciate one another's talents and abilities and use ours to help others. After all, we belong to each other!

by Carolyn Larsen

0-382-30647-3